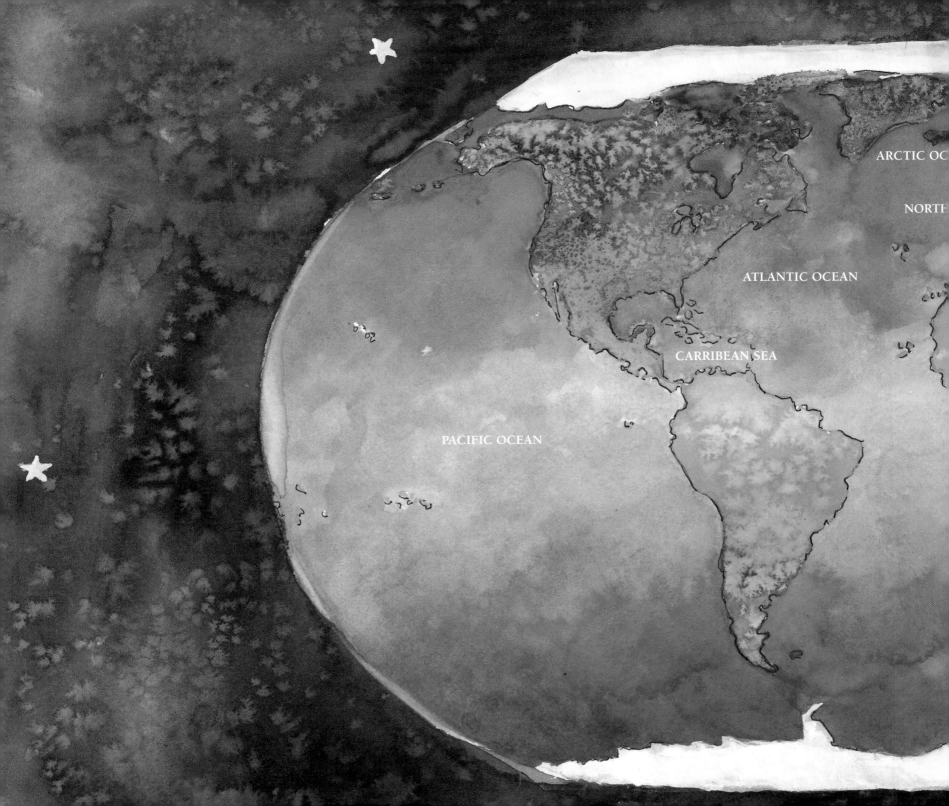

ARCTIC OC

NORTH

ATLANTIC OCEAN

CARRIBEAN SEA

PACIFIC OCEAN

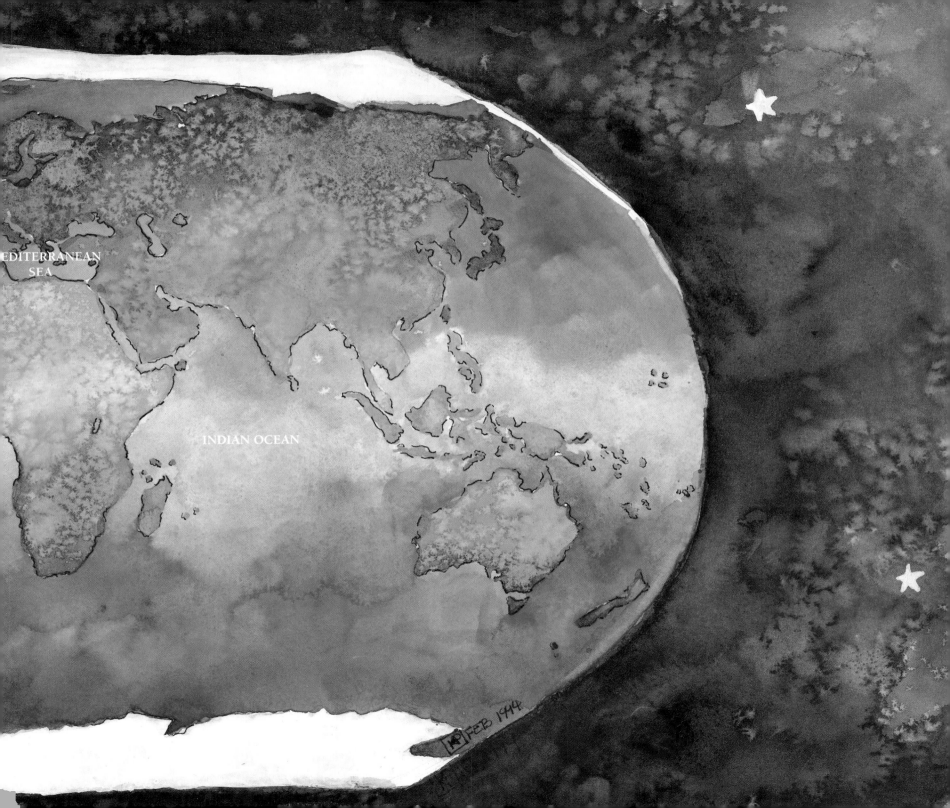

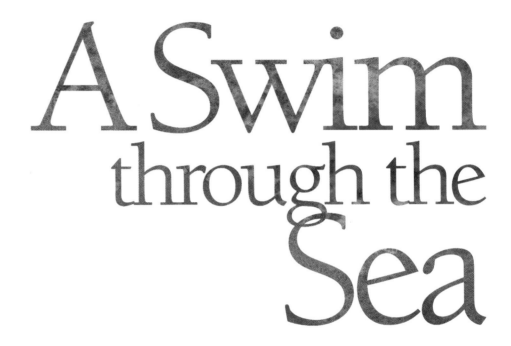

A Swim
through the
Sea

Dedication

To the children of the Blue Planet — may we
work together to protect and preserve its
beauty and diversity.

Published by DAWN Publications
14618 Tyler Foote Road,
Nevada City, CA 95959
916-292-3482

Library of Congress Cataloging-in-Publication Data
Pratt, Kristin Joy.
A Swim through the Sea / written and
illustrated by Kristin Joy Pratt.—1st ed—
Nevada City, CA : Dawn Publications, 1994
[ca. 48]p. : col ill. ; 23 x 27 cm.
ISBN 1-883220-03-3: $16.95 ($24.50 Can.)
ISBN 1-883220-04-1: $7.95 ($11.50 Can.)
1. Marine fauna—Juvenile literature.
2. Marine animals. 3. Alphabet.   I. Title.
QL122.2P73   1994   574.92

Printed on recycled paper using soy based ink
Printed in Hong Kong

10 9 8 7 6 5

Designed by LeeAnn Brook
Type style is Berkeley

Introduction

Water covers two-thirds of the Earth's surface. The oceans contain 97% of this water. Here, some three billion years ago, began the miracle of life. To this day, every living organism contains salt water and is dependent on water for survival.

In the same way that rainforests are referred to as the lungs of our planet, the network of rivers, lakes, and oceans can be thought of as the Earth's circulatory system. First, heat causes water to evaporate. These water vapors accumulate in the atmosphere as clouds, return to the earth as rain or snow, and eventually flow back to the seas. This process, known as the water cycle, cools the Earth's atmosphere and is essential in regulating the planet's temperature.

Among the ocean's varied habitats, coral reefs are especially important, providing homes for more than one quarter of all marine species. Reefs are found only at shallow depths in tropical regions of the world, and cover only a tiny fraction of the ocean floor, an area roughly equal to the size of Texas. Unfortunately, like the rainforests, coral reefs are among the most endangered ecosystems in the world.

Perhaps because man lives on land, he perceives it to be more important than the sea. This, however, is not the case. Interdependence is Earth's ingenious blueprint for survival. Each species needs others to survive; none can exist alone. Each food web within every ecosystem operates on this principle. Energy producing plants are eaten by animals known as herbivores, which are in turn eaten by meat-eaters, known as carnivores. When animals die, their bodies are recycled by bacteria into soil for the plants.

As human beings, we in turn need the oceans for our survival. The oceans provide food for many people and are our largest commercial highway. The sea affects all aspects of our lives, creating floods and rains, and, by withholding water, bringing about droughts. Yet the ocean remains relatively unexplored by man in comparison with terrestrial environments. We are only beginning to understand the workings of this last and largest of the Earth's frontiers.

In the past we have taken our oceans for granted. Now we are finding there is a limit to the amount of garbage and toxic waste we can add to the sea, and to the number of species we can remove from it, before serious harm occurs. The oceans are not infinitely forgiving, and cannot tolerate man's abuse forever. We must work, then, to preserve intact the delicate balance of the ocean's colossal forces. We must look farther ahead than tomorrow before making decisions that affect the stability of the entire globe. Indeed, to quote Captain Jacques Cousteau, "Our liquid future depends upon the foresight, the care, and the love with which we will manage our only water supply: the Oceans."

Kristin Joy Pratt
1994

If Seamore the seahorse,
who lives beneath
the sea,
one day went exploring,
what do you think
he'd see?

He'd admire an amiable **Angelfish** in appealing apparel,

Angelfish are named for their wide, wing-like fins. Among the many colorful species, the queen angelfish, like this one, are by far the most spectacular. Queen angelfish live in the warm tropical waters of the western Atlantic. They are active during the day, when their brilliant markings provide excellent camouflage against the colorful coral reefs. At night they hide in rock crevices. Their flat bodies allow them to slip easily through gaps in the coral. Some angelfish may be as small as your hand; others are as large as this book. To eat, they use their strong teeth to pull off pieces of sponge, coral, and microscopic plants called algae. Like parrots, swans, and a few other animals, angelfish mate for life.

and bump into bright **Blue Crabs**.

Blue crabs are three to nine inches wide with an olive-colored oval shell, or carapace. They get their name from their bright blue legs. As with most crustaceans, the eyes of blue crabs are perched on short flexible stalks. The two pairs of antennae, which are used for smelling and feeling, are actually extensions of their brains.

B

C

He could confront a crazy-colored Clownfish,

The clownfish gets its name from its bright coloring and the downward turn of its mouth. In what is called a symbiotic relationship, the clownfish has a unique partnership with the anemone, a stationary animal with rows of poisonous tentacles around its mouth. The clownfish protects its eggs from predators by laying them at the base of the anemone, in turn, it helps to feed the anemone. The clownfish is protected from the stings of its host by a mucus coating which covers its scales. White bands on its body provide camouflage when it hides among the tentacles of the anemone.

Atlantic Deep Sea Scallops

Drill Shell

Red Drum

Deep Sea Shrimp

Dragonet

D

Drupe Shell

Discus Fish

Dwarf Gourami

Dealfish

Dwar

or discover a dozen delightful **Dolphins** diving up and down.

Dolphins, like all mammals, bear live young and breathe air. Bottlenose dolphins, the largest of the beaked dolphins, grow to be eight to twelve feet long. They live world-wide in temperate and tropical waters, usually in coastal areas, but sometimes in mid-ocean as well. Bottlenose dolphins show a high degree of intelligence, and are very social. They usually have their babies between spring and fall, and have been known to live for 37 years. In the wild, dolphins have often been observed swimming with schools of yellowfin tuna. The exact reason for this relationship is not yet clear to humans.

He'd even encounter an exotic **Eel**,

Moray eels have snake-like bodies up to nine feet long. Their shape enables them to slip in and out of small openings in their rocky reef habitats. Most morays hunt in the evening or at night, finding their food through an excellent sense of smell. During the day morays rest in rock crevices. Morays are generally aggressive, but when handled correctly by divers, they have been known to become very gentle and playful.

E

and find phosphorescent Flashlight fish!

Flashlight fish live in the dark waters of the deep ocean. Under each eye, the fish have a pouch known as a photophore. Each photophore is filled with billions of bacteria that give off a greenish light. The light is a by-product of the bacteria's metabolism, much like heat given off by people when they exercise. This living light is called bioluminescence. Flashlight fish use photophores to see in the dark water, to attract prey and mates, and to frighten or confuse predators. They turn their lights on and off by covering or uncovering the pouches with flaps of skin that act like eyelids for their photophores.

F

G

He'd greet a gargantuan Grouper gladly getting groomed,

Groupers live in the coral reefs of the Caribbean and the Indo-Pacific seas. When they are hungry, they blend in with their surroundings to wait for food. When a crustacean or tasty fish gets close, the grouper snaps open its giant mouth. This quick motion creates a vacuum, sucking in the victim. Groupers also have broad tails. As they spring into action, the first stroke of the tail is so powerful that it creates a sonic boom! During the day, cleaner shrimp, like the one on this grouper, gather to form cleaning stations. Fish visit them and the shrimp eat their parasites. The fish get clean and the shrimp get a free meal.

and hail a happily-housed **Hermit Crab** hobbling along.

Most hermit crabs protect their soft abdomens by living in the empty shells of whelks and other marine snails. When the crab grows too big for one shell, it simply moves into a larger one. Some crabs live in coral tubes or hollow pieces of wood instead of shells. The crab's bright dots provide camouflage in the colorful coral reef. Like all crabs, the hermit crab has ten legs. It uses its huge claw for fighting, catching food, and protecting its shell from attackers. Some hermit crabs provide a kind of mobile home for as many as ten anemones, which attach themselves to the shells. The anemones feed on the crab's leftovers, while the crab is protected from predators by the anemones' poisonous tentacles.

He'd inspect an interesting **Icon Star**,

Because of their bright colors, icon sea stars are very easy to identify. They are omnivores, which means that they eat both plants and animals. Icon stars can grow to be four inches wide, and usually live at depths of 30 to 150 feet. They make their homes throughout the Indo-Pacific region, where they find homes on rocky ocean floors, in channels between reefs, and under coral slabs. Divers often miss seeing these colorful sea stars because there is less light at these depths than near the surface.

Jacknife Cartagena

Jenneria Pustulata

Bar Jack

Junonia

John Dory

J

and join a jet-propelled Jellyfish for a jolly jaunt.

Jellyfish have round, soft, transparent bodies called umbrellas. Although jellyfish have no fins, they do not merely drift with the ocean currents. Instead, they are free-swimming animals that move by jet propulsion. The jellyfish opens its umbrella, drawing in water, then closes it quickly. Water squirts out and creates pressure, sending the jellyfish forward. Jellyfish use long, poisonous tentacles to capture fish. For pink jellyfish these tentacles can be 100 feet long.

Bar Jack

Jenneria Pustulata

Jacknife Cartagena

K

He'd keep a close eye on a creeping crimson **Kelp Crab**,

The kelp crab lives in forests of giant kelp that grow along the coasts of California, Brittany, and South America. The kelp crab occupies the mid-water and upper portion of the plant, where it finds food and protection in the dense growth. More than 800 species of marine animals can live in one healthy forest of giant kelp. A single plant may sustain more than a million organisms. The kelp plant, when harvested and processed, prevents crystals from forming in ice cream and gives paint and toothpaste a creamy texture. Extracts from brown kelp are found in over 300 products used by people. Fortunately, giant kelp recovers rapidly from harvesting, growing one to two feet every day.

and look at lots of lovely little **Limpets**.

Limpets are shelled animals that live in intertidal zones of many temperate rocky coasts. During high tide, they move about underwater to feed on algae. During low tide, however, they are left exposed to air and are in danger of desiccation, which means drying up. Although some organisms in the intertidal zone can survive more than 50 percent desiccation, limpets protect themselves by carving out small hollows, or scars, that match the shape of their shells. As the tide goes out, the limpets fit themselves into their scars, trapping precious water inside their shells.

Moseley's Ascidian

M

Maritime Chromodoris

Seamore might meet many munching **Manatees**,

Manatees have been around for about 45 million years. Like their distant relatives the elephants, they are mammals that breathe air and have little hair. Manatees are herbivores and eat about 100 pounds of sea plants daily. With such a diet, it is no wonder that these gentle giants can weigh up to 3,500 pounds and reach ten to thirteen feet in length. Manatees spend most of their time eating and playing in the warm waters off Florida. Because they are very docile and have fanlike tails, some people believe manatees may have given rise to the mermaid legend. Manatees have no natural enemies, but are often hurt or killed by careless humans in motorboats.

notice a noble **Nautilus** navigating through the nautical night,

The chambered nautilus has existed for 450 million years. It got its name from the numerous compartments in its shell, which enable it to move vertically through 1,000 feet of ocean. To rise, the nautilus fills the chambers with gas; to sink, it absorbs the gas back into its body, filling the shell with water. To move horizontally, the nautilus contracts its body, allowing water to enter its shell. Then by expanding its body, it pushes the water out through a tube called a siphon. This jet-like movement thrusts the nautilus through the water. Like a "living submarine," the nautilus spends its days deep in the ocean, and feeds near the surface at night.

N

O

or ogle an odd-looking Octopus.

The octopus prefers to be alone and likes to hide inside its rocky home. It uses its eight arms for feeding, tasting, and walking. It is very clever, with an ability to learn and remember things. The octopus feeds primarily on crabs and shellfish, using its beak and drill-like tongue to bore holes in their shells. Most species show their moods by turning from silver to brilliant pink when disturbed. If threatened, it squirts out a black, inky cloud to temporarily blind and confuse the predator, allowing the octopus time to escape.

Precious Wenteltrap

Purse Sponge

Pen Shell

Portuguese Man of War

P

He'd peer at a pokey, puffed-up **Porcupine Fish,**

Porcupine fish are small and sluggish, and live mainly in tropical seas. When deflated, they look much like other fish, except for their very large eyes. As soon as danger approaches, they quickly swallow water and balloon to two or three times their size. If suddenly taken from the water, they can inhale air to produce the same effect. When danger is past, they slowly deflate, resuming a normal appearance. Pufferfish, which can also inflate, are closely related to porcupine fish, but have shorter spines. Another close relative, the burrfish, has spines that are always semi-erect.

and quickly peek at a quiet **Queen Conch**.

The queen conch inhabits warm, shallow waters. Generally, it moves slowly on top of the sand, feeding on sea grasses and other marine algae. The conch moves so slowly, in fact, that various marine animals and plants grow on its shell. Although the outside of the shell is rough and crusty, the inside is a beautiful, rosy sunset color. One end of the shell is upturned, allowing the conch to see as it feeds. At the other end is a claw-like operculum, or foot, which it uses to vault away from danger.

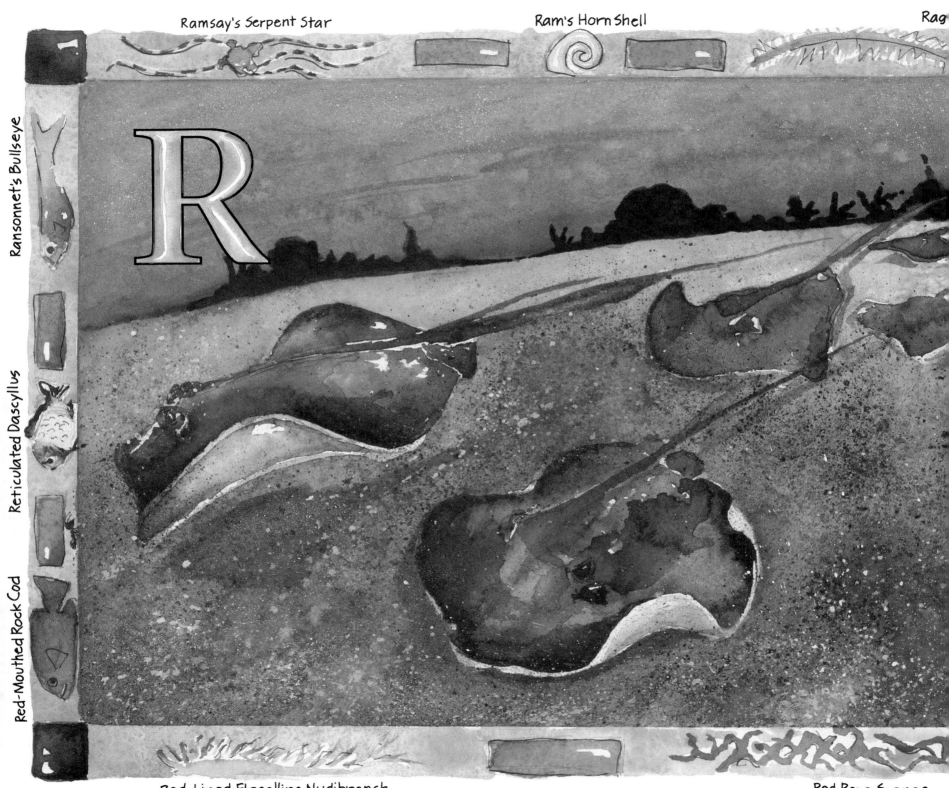

Ramsay's Serpent Star

Ram's Horn Shell

Rag

Ransonnet's Bullseye

Reticulated Dascyllus

Red-Mouthed Rock Cod

R

Red-Lined Flagellina Nudibranch

Red Rope Sponge

Red-Winged Pearl Shell

Red-Spined Sea Urchin

Red Sea Squirt

He'd rapidly recognize **Rays** rippling round a reef,

Most rays are solitary, bottom-dwelling creatures. They hide in the sand during the day, then hunt for squid and other small fish at night. Rays are often colored brown or gray, and blend in with their surroundings. The tails of all rays are long and thin, but some have a poisonous barb protruding from the base. Rays with these special tails are known as stingrays and use their barbs for protection against predators. The rays shown here are southern stingrays. They are swimming in a part of the Caribbean Sea known as "Stingray City," near the island of Grand Cayman. There, the normally solitary rays swim in large groups, and are very active during the daytime. The rays in Stingray City are amazingly gentle as well.

and suddenly spy seven swaying sibling **Seahorses!**

The seahorse is a curious animal about five inches long. Its head has a horse-like look, but the resemblance ends there. It has straw-like jaws, and eyes that move independently, allowing it to look two ways at once. It can even change color to match its habitat. The seahorse is a very weak swimmer and must beat its tiny dorsal fin up to 30 times a second to propel itself. To keep from being carried away by currents, the seahorse uses its tail to grasp sea plants or coral. Because it has no stomach in which to store food, the seahorse eats continuously, consuming as many as 3,500 shrimp daily.

S

Ocellate Thorny Oyster False Trumpet Shell Thick Top Shell   Umbilical Trochid   Channeled Tun

T

He would tarry, talking to a terrific tawny Turtle,

Each year female turtles deposit their eggs in the sand above the high-water mark. Although this practice protects the eggs and hatchlings from the nest-robbers of the deep, it exposes them to land predators such as coconut crabs and frigate birds. Too often, humans join in this assault. It is imperative for the survival of turtles that their main nesting sites be designated as protected sanctuaries. Hatching takes place generally at night, about eight weeks after the eggs are laid. Interestingly, when the temperature of the nest is low, the turtles hatch as males. When the nest is warmer, they hatch as females.

Ocellate Thorny Oyster False Trumpet Shell Thick Top Shell Umbilical Trochid Channeled Tun

Channeled Tun   Umbilical Trochid   Thick Top Shell   False Trumpet Shell   Ocellate Thorny Oyster

U

and uncover unnumbered unusual Urchins.

Although sea urchins differ greatly in size, shape, and texture, they all have spines. These spines are formidable defensive weapons and some are even poisonous. Nevertheless, urchins are preyed upon by fish, crabs, snails, and sea otters. People eat them as well. Since the days of ancient Greece and Rome, sea urchins have been served as a Mediterranean delicacy. Today they are commonly eaten in Japan as sushi. Urchins, themselves, feed mostly on algae. They live in solid or rocky environments such as coral reefs, rock pools, and deep ocean floors.

V

He'd view a **Violetsnail**, vigilant for victuals,

Rather than crawl along the ground, the violetsnail builds a floating "raft" of mucus-coated bubbles and drifts with wind and ocean currents. As it drifts, it hangs suspended from the raft, with its proboscis and forked feelers pointed toward the surface where food is found. The violetsnail eats two types of jellyfish: the Portuguese man-of-war, and the by-the-wind-sailor. Oddly, the violetsnail seems to be immune to the poisonous Portuguese man-of-war, and appears to mimic it by emitting streams of violet dye.

and watch, beneath whipping waves, a wise and wondrous **Whale**.

There are more than sixteen whale species, ranging in size from the nine-foot dolphin to the 100-foot blue whale. Whales have two ways of eating. Toothed whales use their teeth to catch fish and squid. Baleen whales, like this humpback, have a wall of bristly slats that grow from the upper jaw. After taking in large quantities of sea water and tiny organisms, they strain the liquid out through this "baleen" and swallow the tiny animals left behind. Humpbacks are found in all oceans, but migrate between polar waters in summer and tropical waters in winter. Almost 50 feet long, they commonly swim in groups of four to twelve. The humpback emits long, ethereal songs which echo across entire ocean basins and can last for twenty minutes.

He would examine a **Xiphosuran**, exhibiting an excellent example of an exoskeleton,

Xiphosuran (pronounced "zif-a-SOOR-en") is a scientific name for horseshoe crabs. More closely related to spiders than to crabs, these living fossils are remnants of a group of sea creatures that flourished some 200 million years ago. Ranging in size from six to twenty-four inches, these harmless animals migrate into shallow waters to mate. If they cannot move to deeper water before the tide recedes, they bury themselves in the sand to wait for the next high tide. Their hard shells keep them from drying out in the sun.

X

Y

yield to yards and yards of Yellowfin Tuna,

The eggs of yellowfin tuna are the size of pinheads. Just two days after they are laid, the hatchlings emerge. The young have enormous appetites and can gain up to 60 pounds in one year. Adults may reach nearly seven feet in length and may weigh up to 400 pounds. The tapered shape of the yellowfin allows for maximum underwater speed. When fishermen use old-fashioned nets to catch tuna, they also trap or injure the dolphins that swim with the yellowfins. Newer types of nets can trap the tuna while allowing the dolphins to escape. Public concern over the fate of the dolphins has prompted many tuna packagers to market this kind of "dolphin-safe" tuna.

Yellow Commensal Zoanthid

Robust Zoanthid

Zebrasomas Scopas

Z

and zip away from a zapping **Zebrafish!**

The zebrafish inhabits shallow warm waters around reefs and rocks. It is found from the Red Sea through the Indian Ocean to Australia and the Pacific. Its brightly colored pectoral fins are its most distinctive feature. The zebrafish can grow to be 12 inches in length, and has long spines on its back. These dorsal spines carry the deadliest poison of any fish and provide protection from predators. The zebrafish spends its time hiding in reefs or between bottom growths with its fins folded, waiting for unsuspecting prey. When a small fish swims nearby, the zebrafish darts forward with lightning speed to capture its prey. No wonder Seamore is in such a hurry to zip away!

So, swimming back home
on a bright sunny day,
Seamore the seahorse
would certainly say:
"I'm amazed at the beauty
I've seen on the way,
and surely expect
that's the way it will stay.
But it's going to take you,
and it's going to take me,
to keep it a beautiful,
colorful sea."

About the Author

A published book is the dream of every aspiring author. Producing two books before you graduate from high school is a truly extraordinary accomplishment. For 17 year old Kristin Joy Pratt this achievement is the fruit of her belief that anything is possible if you devote sufficient time and energy, and refuse to be distracted by limiting thoughts.

When *A Walk in the Rainforest* was published during her sophomore year, "Parents Magazine" called it "a stunning alphabet book." "School Library Journal" said the book "shows talent and concern". Since then Kristin has maintained a full high school schedule of activities while writing and illustrating *A Swim Through the Sea*. In her "spare" time Kristin has done several tours, speaking at a variety of conferences and bringing her message of environmental concern to large numbers of school children. Both through her books and in her personal life, Kristin is an outstanding role model for today's young people.

Acknowledgments

I would like to express my grateful appreciation to the many friends and family members who have helped make this work possible — especially Janita Lindsay, Marcia Martin, Theodore Munnecke, Kathy Pratt, Katie Pratt, Ken Pratt, Kevin Pratt, Jack Schlueter, and the fine staff at Dawn Publications for their patience and guidance.

ARCTIC OC

NORTH

ATLANTIC OCEAN

CARRIBEAN SEA

PACIFIC OCEAN